World Leaders

QUEEN ELIZABETH II

rourke biographies

World Leaders

QUEEN ELIZABETH II

by
SUSAN AUERBACH

Rourke Publications, Inc.
Vero Beach, Florida 32964

∞ The paper used in this book conforms to the American National Standard for Permanence of Paper for Printed Library Materials, Z39.48-1984.

Library of Congress Cataloging-in-Publication Data
Auerbach, Susan, 1956-
    Queen Elizabeth II / written by Susan Auerbach.
        p.   cm. — (Rourke biographies. World leaders)
    Includes bibliographical references and index.
    Summary: Explores the life of the present British queen, discussing her royal upbringing, the job she inherited, her popularity, commitment to the Commonwealth, and highly publicized family.
    ISBN 0-86625-481-1 (alk. paper)
    1. Elizabeth II, Queen of Great Britain, 1926-   —Juvenile literature.   2. Great Britain—Kings and rulers—Biography—Juvenile literature.   [1. Elizabeth II, Queen of Great Britain, 1926-   . 2. Kings, queens, rulers, etc.]   I. Title. II. Series.
DA590.A87   1993
941.085—dc20   92-46478
                                                                  CIP
                                                                  AC

PRINTED IN THE UNITED STATES OF AMERICA

Contents

950258

Color Illustrations

World Leaders

QUEEN ELIZABETH II

Chapter 1

Ancient Symbol in a Modern World

When Queen Elizabeth II walked slowly down the nave of London's Westminster Abbey to receive the crown in 1953, she was reenacting a ceremony more than one thousand years old. She arrived at church in the same gold coach and bent her head for the same diamond-studded crown that had been used in the coronations of centuries of British rulers before her. But in one important way, Elizabeth's Coronation was dramatically different: it was one of the first major events to be covered by television. Her every move was watched by millions around the world. The Queen had entered the living rooms of ordinary people.

The carrying on of ancient traditions with the help of modern technology was to mark the Queen's long reign. She allowed television coverage of her family life and work in behind-the-scenes documentaries. She took full advantage of the "jet age" to log more than 800,000 miles on official state visits to most parts of the world. All this has brought Queen Elizabeth II closer to the people and made her known to a wider public than any previous king or queen. In the process, she has changed the image of royalty.

A Popular but Powerless Leader

In the forty years that she has been on the throne, Elizabeth has become one of the best known and most loved of world leaders. She reigns over 100 million people (the population of Britain, its dependencies, and fifteen other nations). She is also

The Coronation of Queen Elizabeth II. (AP/Wide World Photos)

Head of the Commonwealth, an association of fifty countries (most of them former British colonies) with a total population of more than one billion people. She has created a role for herself as an energetic goodwill ambassador for both Britain and the Commonwealth.

While other public figures are famous for their actions and abilities, the Queen is simply famous for who she is. Like a movie star, she gets a lot of media coverage, attracts millions of fans, and is very rich. Enthusiastic crowds greet her wherever she goes, from the streets of London to the tiny islands of the Pacific.

Why is the Queen so popular? It seems to be because of a combination of her personal traits and the magic of royalty. The line of British kings and queens dates back eleven hundred years to a time when they were worshipped almost like gods. Today the Queen still inspires some of the same awe among the people who meet her. She is seen as superhuman, yet also as ordinary, "just like us." She is admired because she performs her royal duties with grace, intelligence, and good humor.

The Queen's duties are mostly formal and ceremonial. For example, she approves laws made in Parliament and attends events like the openings of bridges and hospitals. She reigns but does not rule; others conduct the business of government in her name. She holds the traditional royal rights to advise and to warn members of the government. Elizabeth is said to be extremely well-informed about current events. However, she holds no political power and is supposed to be neutral on all matters of controversy.

Why have a queen if she has no power? It may be this powerlessness that makes the British people so loyal to the Queen. Since she does not take sides, she can be respected by people of all sides and accepted as a leader for the whole country. She can be seen as the rudder of the ship of State,

A regal Princess Elizabeth as a baby. (AP/Wide World Photos)

keeping Britain on a steady course that prevents political crises and extremes. More important, the Queen can serve as a symbol of national heritage and unity—the past living on in the present.

The Queen as a Symbol

The Queen's life story is the story not only of a person but of a symbol. She represents the British Crown and the ancient system of monarchy (a government headed by a king or queen who inherits the throne). It is in what she represents, rather than in what she does, that her real power lies.

The monarchy means different things to different people in Britain today. Generally it is a source of national pride. It stands for an ideal of Britain that is noble, continuous, and stable—for everything that is dignified. This dignity is seen at its height in the pomp and pageantry of royalty, such as coronations and royal weddings, which make a great impression on the world.

To a small group of Britons, the monarchy is an unfair system of privilege based on birth—a reminder of harsh divisions between the upper and lower classes (rich and poor). This group believes that the monarchy is an outdated symbol that should be scrapped because it is no longer needed and costs the country too much money. However, the vast majority of British people remain loyal to the Crown and cannot imagine life without it.

As Head of the Commonwealth, the Queen is a symbol of unity for the association's diverse member states. She is also a reminder of the former glory of the British Empire. The country's influence may have declined, but as long as there is a dignified monarch on the throne, some believe, British tradition will be respected around the world.

Understanding a Queen's Life

Her famous face appears on British coins and postage stamps. Hundreds of books and even more articles have been written about her. Yet we may never really understand the life behind the image of the Queen. She is set apart from the rest of humanity because she is Queen. She can do no wrong because she is surrounded by the magic or mystique of the monarchy. Her Palace Press Office works hard to maintain this mystery and ensure a positive image for the Queen. Only a few chosen biographers are allowed to see selected royal documents. The Queen does not give interviews.

As a result, we know Elizabeth more as an ideal than as a real person. Most things written about her are sentimentalized and sugarcoated, often based on rumor rather than fact. It is important to take such accounts of the Queen's life with a grain of salt.

The Queen has spent forty years fulfilling a role that is precious, almost sacred to many people. As we explore the Queen's life—her royal upbringing, the job she inherited, her popularity, her commitment to the Commonwealth, and her highly publicized family—we will try to uncover both the mystery and the reality of what it means to be a queen today.

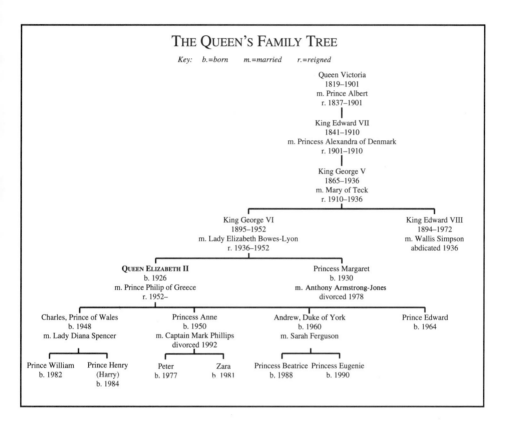

THE QUEEN'S FAMILY TREE

Key: *b.=born*   *m.=married*   *r.=reigned*

Queen Victoria
1819–1901
m. Prince Albert
r. 1837–1901

King Edward VII
1841–1910
m. Princess Alexandra of Denmark
r. 1901–1910

King George V
1865–1936
m. Mary of Teck
r. 1910–1936

King George VI
1895–1952
m. Lady Elizabeth Bowes-Lyon
r. 1936–1952

King Edward VIII
1894–1972
m. Wallis Simpson
abdicated 1936

QUEEN ELIZABETH II
b. 1926
m. Prince Philip of Greece
r. 1952–

Princess Margaret
b. 1930
m. Anthony Armstrong-Jones
divorced 1978

Charles, Prince of Wales
b. 1948
m. Lady Diana Spencer

Princess Anne
b. 1950
m. Captain Mark Phillips
divorced 1992

Andrew, Duke of York
b. 1960
m. Sarah Ferguson

Prince Edward
b. 1964

Prince William
b. 1982

Prince Henry
(Harry)
b. 1984

Peter
b. 1977

Zara
b. 1981

Princess Beatrice
b. 1988

Princess Eugenie
b. 1990

The Queen's Family Tree

Queen Elizabeth was born into her position as Queen. She is the fortieth monarch of England since William the Conqueror in 1066. Her branch of the royal family is known as the Descendants of Queen Victoria or, since King George V, the House of Windsor. This diagram shows some of her ancestors since 1817 and direct descendants up to 1992.

Chapter 2

Growing Up Royal

From the day of her birth on April 21, 1926, in London, Elizabeth's life was a matter of public interest. A government official was on hand to verify and announce that the Duchess of York had given birth to a princess. Fourteen months later, Princess Elizabeth Alexandra Mary made her first public appearance on the balcony of Buckingham Palace, waving to the cheering crowds below with her grandparents, King George V and Queen Mary.

The Princess was born into a world still recovering from World War I. The country's economy was in trouble and more and more people were losing their jobs. Increasing numbers of workers joined trade unions to defend their rights; a General Strike broke out when Elizabeth was twelve days old. All British men over twenty-one and women who met certain conditions had been given the right to vote in 1918; women would not receive full voting rights until 1928. The British Empire Exhibition of 1924 drew seventeen million visitors to its display of "the wondrous reality of Britain's might and magnitude" overseas. Yet the empire was already shrinking and being turned into a voluntary Commonwealth.

No one expected that Princess Elizabeth would come to be the Queen who headed Britain and the Commonwealth. She was third in line for the throne after her uncle, the Prince of Wales, and her father, the Duke of York. If her uncle had children or she had a brother, she would be even further away from the throne. If not for her uncle's surprising abdication (giving up the throne) and her father's untimely death, Elizabeth's life would have been very different.

Royal Role Models: Parents and Grandparents

King George V (reigned 1910-1936) set an example to Elizabeth as an ordinary man who became a beloved father-figure to his people. He was the first monarch to visit coal mines and soccer stadiums, places important to the lives

Princess Elizabeth at the age of one, during a ride on the grounds of Windsor Castle. (AP/Wide World Photos)

of working people. He was also the first to use the mass media (an annual Christmas speech on the radio) to become more familiar to the public. His wife, Queen Mary, set the family's standard for formal, rigidly correct royal behavior.

Though the King was affectionate with Elizabeth, he had

been strict and distant with his son, Prince Albert. Elizabeth's father grew up feeling inferior to his more charismatic older brother. Albert suffered from a stutter and was often ill. Still, he managed to serve in the navy in World War I and step into the role of king when needed. Though never as popular as his father, King George VI (as Albert was known when he became King) was respected for sharing the danger of his people during World War II. His courage and strong sense of duty were passed on to Elizabeth.

In 1922, Prince Albert married Lady Elizabeth Bowes-Lyon, a lovely and lively woman from an old aristocratic family in Scotland. As Duke and Duchess of York, the couple were often away on official tours. Yet they created a close, loving family life for Elizabeth and their second daughter, Margaret Rose. Both parents were to play an important part in the education of the future queen.

A Charmed Childhood

Though she did not live in a palace until she was ten, Elizabeth had a charmed childhood set apart from the real world. She did not know other children except for her royal relatives, whom she saw on holidays or formal occasions. If she went to the park and was recognized, a crowd would form and she would have to go away. An outing on a public bus was a rare, thrilling experience.

Lilibet, as she was known to her family, grew up extremely close to her younger sister Margaret. They shared pillow fights and playthings such as the thirty toy horses which they unsaddled every night. The two girls were dressed alike for many years and became the darlings of the British people. Their faces appeared on postage stamps and chocolate boxes. The people of Wales gave them a miniature thatched cottage to use as a playhouse.

Like other aristocratic parents, the Duke and Duchess of

King George V, Elizabeth's grandfather, the monarch of Great Britain at the time of her birth. (AP/Wide World Photos)

York hired nannies and governesses to take care of their children. One of Elizabeth's nursery maids, known as Bobo, has been with her since the age of four and is still the Queen's confidante and personal attendant. Her governess, Marion "Crawfie" Crawford, later wrote a memoir called *The Little Princesses* which embarrassed the Royal Family.

Elizabeth and Margaret had private lessons with Crawfie in the mornings, then spent the afternoons at sports or artistic pursuits. Their mother taught them to read and tutored them in French and religion. In the Duchess' view, the point of a proper education for her girls was "to spend as long as possible in the open air, to enjoy to the full the pleasures of the country, to be able to dance and draw and appreciate music, to acquire good manners and perfect deportment, and to cultivate all the distinctively feminine graces."

The Princess' greatest pleasure as a child was her pet dogs and horses. Elizabeth was given her own horse at the age of three and a half; by the time she was five, she was taking riding lessons. When she was not riding a real horse, she often played at riding a pretend one. Asked what she wanted to be when she grew up, she replied "a lady in the country with lots of dogs and horses."

To the Palace

Lilibet's simple ambition was not to be. Instead she was thrust into the limelight in 1936, the Year of Three Kings. In one year, her grandfather King George V died; her uncle David, the Prince of Wales, succeeded to and then abdicated the throne; and her father became King.

The Princess' uncle, who became known as King Edward VIII, was impatient with the formality and model behavior expected of royalty. When he wanted to marry an American woman, Wallis Simpson, who had been divorced twice, there was an uproar in the British Royal Family and the government.

Princess Elizabeth on her fourteenth birthday, celebrated at Windsor. (AP/ Wide World Photos)

The Church of England, of which the King was Supreme Governor, prohibited divorce and could not approve the marriage. The King was advised that he would have to either give up his marriage plans or give up the throne. He did the latter in a farewell speech which shocked the nation on December 11, 1936. This was a lesson to the little princess in how not to be a king, suggests biographer Robert Lacey.

It was also how Elizabeth's father, the next in line for the throne, came to be King George VI—a job he never wanted. "Does that mean you will have to be the next Queen?" Margaret asked her sister. "Yes, some day," Elizabeth replied. "Poor you," said Margaret, aware that a queen's life is not her own.

The family moved into Buckingham Palace, a maze of 602 rooms with private apartments, ornate reception halls, and offices built in 1825. "People here need bicycles," remarked Elizabeth of the palace's miles of carpeted corridors. The little princesses mixed with children of palace officials in Brownie and Girl Guide troops formed just for them.

The family remained close, playing cards or charades when there was time. King George VI called his family "the Royal Firm," comparing them to a business enterprise. He took to his work conscientiously and expected the others to do the same.

Groomed for the Crown

Elizabeth's first important lesson in her future role as Queen was studying her father's Coronation ceremony in 1937. The King gave her a specially bound book with the order of the religious service. Her grandmother, determined that Elizabeth learn how royalty should behave, often took the Princess with her to public engagements at galleries and hospitals.

Elizabeth had had very little formal education until this time—only about one and a half hours a day with her governess or French tutors. Now she was given her own history tutor, Sir Henry Marten of Eton College, a prestigious boarding school that has educated many of Britain's leaders. Marten taught Elizabeth about the British constitution and current events with a kind sense of humor and a stress on understanding rather than rote memorizing.

Whenever he was at home, the King discussed the day's events with his oldest daughter on morning walks in the palace grounds or evenings in his study. He impressed on Elizabeth how important it was to serve the nation in the job-for-life of monarch. Gradually he let her see some of the government papers he was sent. He appointed her a counsellor of state when she was eighteen so that she could take over certain duties in his absence, such as signing a pardon for a prisoner.

Meanwhile, the teenage Elizabeth was getting a broader view of the world. She had fallen in love with her third cousin, Prince Philip of Greece, a tall, dashing cadet at naval college. He was full of energy, quick wit, and strong opinions—an exciting contrast to Elizabeth's shyness and protected family life. Well-traveled and worldly, Prince Philip would help her gain confidence as she took on heavier royal duties.

Living through World War II was to have a similar effect on the Princess and to be a crucial step in her job training.

Chapter 3

A Normal Life?

The war years brought the young princess closer than ever before to the concerns of ordinary people in the world outside the palace. Yet she still lived with certain royal privileges and protection.

The main concern of Elizabeth's father's reign (1936-1952) was dealing with the effects of World War II. When fascist governments arose in Germany, Italy, and Spain in the 1930's, Britain tried to stay out of their way. Finally, however, angered by Hitler's invasion of Poland, Britain declared war on Germany in 1939. Prime Minister Winston Churchill led the country through the devastating war to victory for the Allied side in 1945.

In spite of frequent bombings of London, the King and Queen continued to live at Buckingham Palace. They visited heavily hit neighborhoods to show their support, winning the appreciation of the public.

Elizabeth and Margaret were sent to Windsor Castle, where they could be nearby but safer than in London. Like other young people during the war, the princesses ate food and wore clothes that were rationed (sold in limited quantities by coupons) and went underground during air raids. Elizabeth gave a speech on a popular radio program to reassure British children that "all will be well." To pass the time, she took care of her horses and acted in Christmastime productions of plays such as *Aladdin*, much to the amusement of her family. And she wrote letters to Prince Philip, who was serving on a battleship in the Mediterranean Sea.

Nine-year-old Princess Elizabeth with her mother, the Duchess of York, and her younger sister, Princess Margaret Rose. (AP/Wide World Photos)

Second Subaltern Elizabeth Windsor

As the war dragged on, the Princess was impatient to have a part in it "as other girls of my age do." The King was against the idea, even though it was from him that Elizabeth had taken her strong need to serve the country. Finally he allowed her to join the Auxiliary Transport Service (now the Women's Royal Army Corps) in April of 1945. Here she learned to drive and repair heavy military trucks and was known as Second Subaltern Elizabeth Windsor.

Much is made of this episode in biographies of the Queen, with photos showing a young Elizabeth in uniform with tools in hand. But in fact, she stayed with the training course for only a few weeks and always went back to the palace to sleep, rather than staying in the barracks.

Elizabeth's brief stint of war duty was interrupted by VE Day, the official end of the war, on May 8, 1945. Crowds of Londoners ran dancing, singing, and shouting through the streets. The Royal Family appeared on the palace balcony and the princesses were allowed to join the street celebrations, wearing scarves so they would not be recognized.

Engagement and Marriage

Elizabeth accepted Philip's proposal of marriage in 1946 without asking her parents. They were pleased with her choice, but the King was reluctant to break up the "Royal Firm" so soon. He had been looking forward to a family tour of South Africa and decided to delay announcing the engagement until after the trip.

There were also some formalities to be arranged. The marriages of people in line for the throne have always been matters of public concern, subject to government approval. In order to marry the Princess, the Greek-born Philip had to become a naturalized citizen of Britain and to convert from the Greek Orthodox religion to the Church of England.

While in Cape Town, South Africa, the twenty-one-year-old Princess Elizabeth made her famous "coming-of-age" speech. She told radio listeners, "I declare before you that my whole life, whether it be long or short, shall be devoted to your

The wedding of Princess Elizabeth and Prince Philip. (AP/Wide World Photos)

service and the service of our great Imperial Commonwealth, to which we all belong." If she had known then how soon she would be called upon to serve her country, it might have spoiled her excitement about her coming marriage.

The royal wedding in November of 1947 was a grand occasion, with ten thousand pearls sewn into the Princess' white satin gown and fifteen hundred gifts on display. It cheered up the British people, who were still living under wartime restrictions such as the rationing of food and gas.

Wife and Mother

For the next few years, Princess Elizabeth was preoccupied with her own private life—a luxury she would never have again. She gave birth to a son, Charles, in 1948 to great public rejoicing and to a daughter, Anne, in 1950. She made a point of sharing breakfast with her children and bathing them and putting them to bed herself, even if she was busy with royal duties the rest of the day. She wanted to bring up her children "as normally as possible."

Prince Philip, who had been given the title Duke of Edinburgh, was graduated from naval college and took command of his own ship. Elizabeth traveled now for personal reasons: to be with her husband on holiday in Malta, to visit her husband's birthplace in Greece.

Meanwhile, the King was increasingly weak from cancer and unable to travel. He turned over more engagements to his daughter and son-in-law. In January of 1952, the King saw them off on a Commonwealth tour that was soon to be interrupted.

Accession at Treetops

When King George VI died on February 6, 1952, at the age of fifty-six, Elizabeth and Philip were staying at a rustic game lodge called Treetops in the African colony of Kenya. They

Princess Elizabeth holds her son, Prince Charles, after his christening at Buckingham Palace. (AP/Wide World Photos)

had spent the night watching wild elephants and rhinos from their balcony high up in a fig tree, and intended to go fishing. All plans were canceled as the stunned couple arranged to return to Britain for the funeral and ceremonies of accession (succession to the throne). Suddenly, Elizabeth was Queen. She was only twenty-five years old.

On her return home, the new Queen was met at the airport by Prime Minister Churchill and other top politicians. Appearing alone in black mourning clothes, she already showed the calm and seriousness that were to become her royal style. But she must have felt grief both for the loss of her father and the loss of her youth and privacy. She referred to her job as "this heavy task which has been laid upon me so early in my life," but she committed herself to performing it well.

Postwar Britain and the New Commonwealth

Conditions were changing fast around her as the new Queen strived to come up to speed on British politics and world affairs. World War II had transformed Britain and brought people together. Men from rich and poor families had mingled in battles and barracks, while on the home front, large numbers of women joined the work force for the first time. A Labour government elected in 1945 began ambitious housing programs, created the National Health Service, and nationalized key industries. But the war had strained Britain's resources, and it was slower than other Western countries to recover.

Their experience in World War II also made many of the world's peoples impatient to rule themselves. India had always been the "jewel in the crown" of the British Empire. When it finally broke away in 1947, split into two independent states (India and Pakistan), and joined the Commonwealth, it set a pattern for other British colonies. Elizabeth II was the first monarch to be named Head of the Commonwealth, but it was still too soon to know what this would mean.

In 1952, the nation's hopes were focused on the new Queen. There was talk of a New Elizabethan Age in which a revitalized Britain would again take up its leading role in the world. The Conservative Party was back in power under Churchill and preparations for Elizabeth's Coronation seemed to spell a return to glorious tradition.

Chapter 4

The Queen's Inheritance

Elizabeth was now officially "Elizabeth the Second, by the Grace of God of the United Kingdom of Great Britain and Northern Ireland and of Her other Realms and Territories Queen, Head of the Commonwealth, Defender of the Faith." With this cumbersome title, she inherited a job-for-life and the tremendous wealth, traditions, and reputation of the British monarchy.

The Queen set the tone for her reign with preparations for her magnificent Coronation on June 2, 1953. She showed that she would respect tradition and play her part in the colorful pageantry that the people loved. She studied records of past coronations and rehearsed her steps carefully to be sure not to leave anything out of the three-hour ceremony.

Heading the grand procession to Westminster Abbey were dignitaries from around the world. The Queen, in a horse-drawn gold coach, was flanked by the Yeomen of the Guard in sixteenth-century-style red coats and ribboned hats. Behind the coach marched ten thousand soldiers and two thousand bandsmen. Elizabeth's personal beauty added splendor to the solemn ritual at the Abbey. She wore a fur cape over a purple velvet train and a white dress richly embroidered with emblems of the Commonwealth countries. After being presented to the people and taking the Coronation oath, she was anointed with holy oil and dressed in gold robes. She was given the four symbols of monarchy: the orb (for the world ruled by God), the scepter (for royal authority), the rod (for mercy), and the royal ring. Then Britain's chief religious leader, the Archbishop of Canterbury, placed the five-pound

Sociologist Edward Shils describes Elizabeth's Coronation as an "act of national communion," bringing Church and State together in a religious ceremony. (AP/Wide World Photos)

Crown of St. Edward on her head. The cry went out, "God save the Queen!" Trumpets blared, church bells pealed, and guns saluted.

London had been wild with Coronation fever for months. There were Coronation songs, Coronation mugs, and mock-Coronation ceremonies by children at Coronation street parties. Half a million people camped out in the rain the night before just to catch a glimpse of the Queen along the five-mile route. Millions more bought their first televisions for the occasion. Common responses were "It's like fairyland" or "It makes you feel proud to be British." Though some people felt that all the pageantry was too much fuss, the magic of monarchy had most of Britain and the world under its sway.

The Magic of Monarchy

Elizabeth's Coronation was "an act of national communion" that brought Church and State together in a religious ceremony, according to sociologist Edward Shils. This religious element at the center of the monarchy is no accident. Kings and queens in medieval England were treated like gods who had a divine right to rule. Their touch was believed to cure certain illnesses; their political power was absolute.

Modern British monarchs have continued to hold a magical power over their people that is not entirely rational. As recently as 1964, one third of Britons surveyed still believed that the Queen was chosen by God. She has been called "the last thing on earth that is sacred." Indeed, many people worship the Queen, perhaps out of a psychological need for heroes. Certain customs help maintain a sense of mystery around the monarch, such as rules of etiquette that forbid touching her (except a handshake) and official secrecy about her finances. To criticize the Queen is taboo (forbidden), like something sacrilegious.

The monarch and the monarchy are a reflection of how the

British people see themselves. Loyalty to the Crown is at the core of their deep-rooted sense of national identity. Revering the Queen goes along with a general British tendency to idealize whatever is ancient. Elizabeth, who can trace her ancestry to King Edgar in the tenth century, is linked to a nearly unbroken line of kings and queens. The legacy of their rule is also part of her inheritance.

The History of the Monarchy

The English throne has been occupied by a varied group of individual kings and queens. (Britain as we know it today began to take shape in 1603, when King James I unified England, Scotland, and Ireland under one crown.) Some monarchs, such as Queen Elizabeth I in the sixteenth century, left their mark on an entire era (the Elizabethan Age) with their strong leadership, victory in battle, and support of the arts. Others, such as George IV in the nineteenth century, lived extravagantly with no sense of responsibility to their people. A number of English monarchs have been murdered, but only once has their power been disrupted by those opposed to the idea of monarchy.

The English Parliament was created as a representative lawmaking body in the twelfth century. Originally, its members were expected to carry out the will of the monarch. As the power of Parliament grew, that of the monarch weakened. The arrogant Charles I was beheaded by an angry Parliament in 1647 and for a brief time (1649-1660), Britain was a republic without a monarch. The monarchy was restored under Charles II, but by the reign of George I (1714-1727), the ruler was expected to obey the will of Parliament. This arrangement, which limits the monarch's powers, is known as constitutional monarchy.

Modern constitutional monarchy dates from changes during the long reign of Queen Victoria (1837-1901). Like her great-great-granddaughter, the present Queen, Victoria became immensely popular. Her reign saw greater voting rights for the masses, the rise of the middle class, and the most glorious years of the British Empire. Under Victoria's son, Edward VII (reigned 1901-1910), and later under Elizabeth II's grandfather and father, the monarchy came to be seen as a symbol of democracy (rule by the people) rather than aristocracy (rule by the nobility). The more political power it lost, the more symbolic power the monarchy seemed to gain.

The Workings of a Constitutional Monarchy

The Queen inherited a time-honored way of doing things as a constitutional monarch. According to the unwritten British constitution, the monarch, as head of state, invites the Prime Minister to form a government of Cabinet ministers in his or her name. The Queen has certain royal rights and prerogatives (privileges to make a personal choice) that are supposed to be a check on the power of Parliament. These include "the right to be consulted, the right to encourage, and the right to warn" government officials. The Queen must approve all bills passed in Parliament and, theoretically, has the right to veto them; however, no British monarch has used the veto since 1707. She also summons and dissolves Parliament, appoints and dismisses Cabinet members, gives out noble titles, and chooses the Prime Minister. Usually this choice is automatic: the monarch simply sends for the leader of the political party that has the majority of seats in Parliament. To advise her, the Queen has a Privy Council of nearly four hundred members who serve for life.

The Queen is head of state, like the President of the United States, but unlike him, she cannot make policy. The President gives a State of the Union address to Congress, which outlines his plans and reveals his views on important issues. The Queen gives a Queen's Speech to Parliament, but she is only reading

38

The Queen and Her Prime Ministers

*The Queen has worked with nine very different Prime
Ministers in the course of her reign. They are:*

Winston Churchill	1951-1955
Anthony Eden	1955-1957
Harold Macmillan	1957-1963
Alec Douglas Home	1963-1964
Harold Wilson	1964-1970
	1974-1976
Edward Heath	1970-1974
James Callaghan	1976-1979
Margaret Thatcher	1979-1990
John Major	1990-

*The Queen meets with the Prime Minister for an hour
every Tuesday evening. This is so she can stay informed on
important matters of state and "advise and warn" the
government if she sees fit. Her Prime Ministers have
generally been impressed with the Queen's devotion to her
job and knowledge of political affairs.*

*The Queen was brought up to be apolitical (that is, to
have no strong attachment to any political party or faction).
Her best relationships were with Harold Macmillan and
Harold Wilson—one a Tory, the other a leader of the
Labour Party. Her most strained relationships were with
Edward Heath and Margaret Thatcher, who came from
middle-class rather than upper-class backgrounds.
Whatever her personal feelings about her Prime Ministers,
the Queen has made a habit of inviting them to her summer
home at Balmoral, where she serves them tea and washes up
afterward.*

what has been written by government officials about the government's plans; she is not allowed to express her opinion. Instead, she concentrates on ceremonial duties such as greeting new foreign ambassadors and entertaining visiting heads of state at the palace.

The Roles of the Monarch

The Queen fills a variety of roles as head of state (see appendix, "The Queen's Roles"). She is head of important British institutions, including the Church of England, the armed forces, and the legal system. Many things are done "in the Queen's name": declarations of war and peace; the conduct of courts of law; the appointment of officials such as judges, army officers, and church leaders; and the awarding of honors such as knighthoods. Indeed, the Queen is considered the Fount of Honor, giving out medals and honorary titles to more than three thousand people per year. But nearly all these actions are taken on the advice of her ministers and staff, rather than on the Queen's own initiative.

Outside Britain, the Queen's role is even more purely symbolic. In 1952, she was head of state in five countries outside Britain (the realms of Australia, Canada, Ceylon, New Zealand, and South Africa). Today the number stands at fifteen (Antigua and Barbuda, Australia, The Bahamas, Barbados, Belize, Canada, Grenada, Jamaica, New Zealand, Papua New Guinea, St. Christopher and Nevis, St. Lucia, St. Vincent and the Grenadines, Solomon Islands, and Tuvalu), many of them small island states. The Queen is represented by an appointed Governor-General in these realms, but each has a parliament independent of Britain. As Head of the Commonwealth, the Queen makes frequent tours to her realms and to other countries in the Commonwealth "club," getting to know their leaders and problems. But she does not take official part in the discussions at Commonwealth Conferences.

Harold Macmillan, Prime Minister from 1957 to 1963; the Queen learned much from him about international relations. (AP/Wide World Photos)

The Trappings of Monarchy

In order to fulfill her various roles with dignity and efficiency, the Queen is given money, people to help her, and special homes and possessions. These trappings of monarchy are currently supported by the British government at a cost of more than $100 million per year. Part of this amount goes to the Civil List, which is an allowance for the Queen's staff and official duties. The rest goes to such things as security, the support of the Royal Family, and the maintenance of royal property (including three palaces for the Queen, the yacht Britannia, three jets, two helicopters, and fourteen special train cars).

The 350 people who work in the Royal Household help the Queen with ceremonies, visitors, and personal needs. They are sworn to secrecy about whatever they see or hear in the palace. They do everything from catering state dinners for hundreds of diplomats and guarding the Queen on parade, to grooming her horses and sewing her dresses. Several Ladies-in-Waiting help answer the Queen's mail and go with her on tours. A Private Secretary briefs her on daily matters, writes her speeches, plans her travels, and oversees her Press Office.

With her job, the Queen inherited priceless collections that are held in trust for the nation. They include the world's largest private art collection, plus jewelry, postage stamps, and antiques. The Queen also became the owner of lands in the Duchy of Lancaster and the private family estates of Sandringham and Balmoral. With the large income from these lands plus her race horses and investments, Queen Elizabeth is the richest woman in the world. Until 1993, she did not pay any taxes. As we will see, the Queen's tax-free wealth during the first forty years of her reign led to controversy and even to calls by some for an end to the monarchy.

On-the-Job Training

The first years of Elizabeth's reign were a kind of honeymoon period. She went on a six-month tour of Commonwealth countries that boosted the world's romantic image of a fairy-tale Queen. On the Polynesian island of Fiji, for instance, she was toasted with drinks in coconut shells and presented with the gift of a whale's tooth. Upon her return, thousands of cheering Britons welcomed her ship home. More jubilant crowds greeted the Queen and her husband under the banner "Welcome Phil and Liz" during their first visit to the United States in 1957. Elizabeth charmed politicians and won the adoration of a public that was optimistic about a better future. Indeed, after the lean postwar years, Britain was beginning to enjoy a period of greater prosperity.

The young Queen had to learn fast to make up for her lack of political experience. She developed a practical, no-nonsense style of "doing the boxes," going through the boxes of government papers delivered to her each day and giving her approval where needed. She depended heavily on the experience of her early Prime Ministers, with whom she met weekly. She called Harold Macmillan "my guide and supporter through the mazes of international affairs and my instructor in many vital matters." He, in turn, found her "not only very charming but incredibly well-informed" and was amazed at "Her Majesty's grasp of all the details."

Twice in her early years as Queen, Elizabeth set off controversies in her choice of a Prime Minister. At the time, the two main political parties in Parliament were Conservative (also called Tory) and Labour. When Tory Prime Minister (PM) Anthony Eden retired in 1957, his deputy, R. A. Butler, was expected to take over. But Elizabeth summoned Macmillan for the post on the advice of Churchill and the Cabinet. When Macmillan stepped down six years later, the Queen angered some politicians by passing over Butler again in favor of Alec Douglas Home. Home later promoted a bill in Parliament to allow the Tories to elect their own leader as Labour did, rather than depend on the Queen's choice.

Shadows on the New Elizabethan Age

Elizabeth had some other hard lessons in her first decade as Queen. One was watching helplessly as her government was humiliated during the Suez Canal crisis in 1956, when the United States and the United Nations forced Britain to withdraw its troops from Egypt.

Closer at hand, the Queen was personally embarrassed by the fuss caused by her sister's wish to marry Group Captain Peter Townsend, a member of the Royal Household. Princess Margaret needed the Queen's approval to marry, since she was an heir to the throne who was under twenty-five. The Queen was sympathetic. But the government advised her against the match because Townsend was divorced and the Church of England still disapproved of divorce. The whole matter was left in limbo for three years until the anguished Margaret finally gave up Townsend.

In 1957, the Palace and the public were shocked by some sharp criticism of the Queen in the left-wing press. Journalist Malcolm Muggeridge made fun of what he called the "royal soap opera" and the worship of the Queen as "a sort of substitute or ersatz [artificial] religion." Lord Altrincham complained that the Queen was more like a "priggish schoolgirl, captain of the hockey team," than a knowledgeable head of state. Both writers received death threats and hate mail from Crown supporters accusing them of treason.

Modernizing the Monarchy

Clearly, the Queen needed to appear more modern and pay more attention to her public image. The Palace began to make small changes in this direction in the late 1950's. The Queen was coached in more effective speech making and began to give her Christmas Speech on television rather than radio. The exclusive parties for debutantes from high society were canceled. The Queen's son, Prince Charles, became the first member of the Royal Family to go to private school rather than to have lessons at home with tutors. In 1962, the Queen opened her Picture Gallery, marking the first time that the public could enter part of Buckingham Palace. She also began to invite a much wider range of people to luncheons at the palace and to huge summer garden parties.

All of this was meant to show that the Queen was up-to-date and accessible to the people. The building of the Queen's image as a modern, popular monarch was to be the Palace's main concern for the next decade.

Chapter 5

The People's Queen

The Queen owes her tremendous fame and popularity to reigning for so long during the media age. It was during the 1960's that her staff began to use the media expertly to the Queen's advantage.

The media's love affair with royalty actually dates back to the 1880's. New technology made photography easier and gave rise to cheap national newspapers for the masses. After the abdication crisis of the 1930's, women's magazines began running regular articles about the Royal Family. By the New Elizabethan Age, the public's hunger for news and gossip about royals was becoming insatiable.

The Queen had recognized the power of the new medium of television when she went against the advice of her old-fashioned staff and allowed her Coronation to be filmed. Sir Richard Colville, who had been Palace Press Secretary since 1947, thought such publicity was undignified and took away from the glamorous mystique of the monarchy.

When William Heseltine replaced Colville in 1968, however, things began to change. Heseltine and Prince Philip convinced the Queen that if television were used carefully, it could greatly boost her popularity. The trick was to find a balance between too much publicity, which might make her seem too familiar, and too little publicity, which might make her seem distant from the people. In 1969, the Queen agreed to allow the government's British Broadcasting Corporation (BBC) to make a television documentary about her family life.

The Swinging Sixties

The timing of this media event at the height of the Swinging Sixties was no accident. The 1960's began a period of radical social change in Britain, as in other Western countries. After thirteen years of Conservative government, Harold Wilson's Labour Party was elected in 1964. It pledged to improve the country's education system and social services.

Race relations was the explosive issue of the decade. Thousands of immigrants from the West Indies, India, Pakistan, and other parts of the Commonwealth poured into Britain despite government restrictions. If this wave of new settlers continued, warned politician Enoch Powell, there would be "rivers of blood." Demonstrations against nonwhite immigration even reached the palace. At the same time, there were race riots by blacks in Brixton and Liverpool demanding better jobs and housing. In her 1968 Christmas Speech, the Queen pleaded for tolerance between the races.

The 1960's saw the beginnings of a breakdown in old relationships and forms of authority. Students and workers protested against those who made the rules. The Divorce Reform Act of 1969 made it easier for couples who simply were not getting along to get a divorce. The Beatles rock band and the boutiques along Carnaby Street created new fashions of rebellion. Daring television programs such as "That Was the Week That Was" made fun of the Queen and other public figures in a way that would not have been acceptable before. Many young people apparently felt the Queen was stuffy and out of touch with the times.

Meanwhile, an expanded Royal Family had made the public more curious than ever about "what they are really like." The Queen had two more children, Prince Andrew in 1960 and Prince Edward in 1964. Princess Margaret's romance with the photographer Anthony Armstrong-Jones, whom she married in 1960, became the subject of countless stories in the media.

The Queen's Day

A typical day for the Queen at Buckingham Palace begins with tea and newspapers brought to her room by her trusted servant, Bobo. While she has breakfast with her husband, the royal bagpiper plays outside her window. She consults with her private secretary about her schedule and any other pressing matters, then turns to her paperwork.

The Queen spends about two hours a day "doing the boxes," reading through official and sometimes secret papers of the latest Cabinet, Parliament, and Commonwealth business and giving her approval where needed. (The locked leather boxes are sent to her even when she is away on vacation.) She reads and answers some of her mail herself, while her Ladies in Waiting assist her with the rest. The Queen receives about fifty thousand letters a year. Some are requests for her to attend an event; others, which she turns over to the appropriate government office, ask for help on an individual or community problem; still others are fan mail.

Afternoons are filled with luncheons, receptions, audiences (private meetings with individuals), and public engagements. The Queen's schedule is planned one year ahead of time. She might visit a military academy to inspect her troops, appear at opening ceremonies for a new power station, or attend a benefit performance for a charity.

The Queen unwinds by feeding her eleven Corgi dogs and walking them around the palace grounds. Except for when there is a special event or her weekly meeting with the Prime Minister, she tries to reserve evenings for private time at home.

1. The newly crowned Queen Elizabeth II, 1953. (AP/Wide World Photos)

2. Elizabeth and the Duke of Edinburgh (Prince Philip) at her Coronation. (AP/Wide World Photos)

3. The gold coach in which Elizabeth proceeded to her Coronation. (AP/Wide World Photos)

4. The Coronation ceremony in Westminster Abbey. (AP/Wide World Photos)

5. The Queen in the Throne Room of Buckingham Palace, celebrating her Silver Jubilee, 1977. (AP/Wide World Photos)

6. A walkabout near St. Paul's Cathedral during the Silver Jubilee. (AP/Wide World Photos)

7. The Queen, wearing her crown of jewels, 1982. (AP/Wide World Photos)

8. The Queen on her mare Burmese, a gift from the Royal Canadian Mounted Police, at the annual Trooping the Colour ceremony, during the Silver Jubilee. (AP/Wide World Photos)

9. The Royal Family at Windsor Castle in 1968: (from left) Prince Charles, Prince of Wales, Prince Edward, Prince Andrew, Princess Anne, the Queen, and Prince Philip. (AP/Wide World Photos)

10. On the grounds of Buckingham Palace, the Queen reviews her Yeomen of the Guard, 1978. (AP/Wide World Photos)

11. The Queen and Prince Philip with their guests, Queen Beatrix and Prince Claus of the Netherlands, 1982. (AP/Wide World Photos)

12. The Queen and Prince Philip, in a picture taken by Prince Andrew in the drawing room at Sandringham House in Norfolk, 1986. (AP/Wide World Photos)

13. A smile from the Queen, 1991. (AP/Wide World Photos)

The Palace was planning a spectacular ceremony for the investiture (installation in office) of twenty-one-year-old Prince Charles as Prince of Wales in 1969. Since the thirteenth century, presenting their first sons to the people of Wales had been a way for English monarchs to try to win the loyalty of the reluctant Welsh. The Palace hoped that the television documentary would make the public sympathetic toward the Royal Family, and thus set the stage for this important ceremony.

Royal Family: The Movie

A BBC team under producer Richard Cawston spent two and a half months filming the daily lives of the Queen and her family. Their 105-minute documentary, *Royal Family*, was a first in British broadcasting and a brilliant publicity coup for the Palace. For the first time the British public could see the royals talking informally with their children, their staff, and foreign dignitaries rather than making prepared speeches. Britons were fascinated to watch the Queen doing the same things they did—feeding her dogs, preparing a picnic, decorating the Christmas tree. There was her husband turning sausages on the barbecue and little Prince Edward playing in the nursery. More than anything else in her reign, the film convinced many Britons that the Queen and her family were "just like us."

Some anti-monarchists dismissed the film as "a large-scale commercial." If it was meant to "sell" the Royal Family to the public, it did a superb job. The royal image changed overnight. Even young people felt more positive about the Queen after seeing the film, according to opinion polls. Inspired by the film's success, the Palace retained the same camera crew for the Queen's Christmas Speeches, which became more informal, chatty, and family-oriented.

Prince Charles's investiture, also televised, was a stunning show of the monarchy's determination to use the new to uphold the old. Princess Margaret's artistic husband, now known as Lord Snowdon, designed striking, ultra-modern decor for the ancient castle courtyard where the ceremony took place. The media was charmed by the intelligent and well-spoken prince.

"Walkabout"

A year later the Palace found another way to "humanize" the Queen and bring her closer to the people. Until then, the public could only see the waving Queen from a distance during public engagements. In New Zealand in 1970, the Queen broke with tradition to mingle freely with the crowd, chatting and shaking hands. This practice became known as a "walkabout" (from a word used by the Aborigine people of Australia).

Walkabouts removed another barrier between the Queen and her subjects. They also added danger by exposing Elizabeth to direct contact with mobs of people. But the Queen has never been much concerned with security; perhaps she assumes that the dignity of her office is enough protection. She finds it too confining to be surrounded by ranks of bodyguards or isolated behind bulletproof glass, as other heads of state usually are. "I must be seen to be believed," she has said.

Walkabouts became a hallmark of the Queen's more relaxed style, both at home and abroad. Excited crowds vied for a chance to speak with or touch the Queen. Still, they were bound by certain rules of protocol (correct official behavior). Those who meet the Queen are supposed to call her "Ma'am," to bow or curtsey slightly, and to wait for the Queen to speak first or ask the questions. Even little children may not kiss or hug her, but only shake her gloved hand. In spite of these restrictions, those who meet the Queen up close are often struck by her dry sense of humor and her lively interest in people.

The investiture of Prince Charles as Prince of Wales. (AP/Wide World Photos)

The Queen has worn out hundreds of pairs of gloves shaking hands with ordinary people over the years. It cannot be easy facing crowds at more than five hundred public engagements a year. The news reporters who follow the Queen have been impressed with her stamina. She manages to stand for hours at a time and rarely looks bored as she finds an appropriate word or two to say to those around her. She even takes a mischievous delight in making do when small things go wrong. It is a rare chance for spontaneity in a life that is so tightly planned.

The Cult of Personality

The documentary *Royal Family* and Elizabeth's walkabouts drew back some of the secrecy that had always surrounded the monarchy. They revealed glimpses of the Queen as a person rather than just a lofty symbol. The more the British people knew about the Queen, the more they wanted to know. This was especially true for middle-aged and older women in the London area—always the Queen's greatest fans. The press and royal biographers were ready to feed the public's curiosity.

A cult of personality grew up around the Queen, an obsession with her person that glorified everything from her famous hats to her sensible shoes. Here is a teacher's description of one person's fanatic devotion to the Queen and her family: "I have followed the Royal Family since I was seven. I have collected many books, and I have my own album in which I keep newspaper cuttings; these total 2641. My ambition is to meet the Queen, and I hope one day to write a book about her. In fact my whole life revolves round royalty, and were we to become a republic I would pack my bags. . . . I would give my life for the Queen."

Just who is the object of all this interest and adoration? Elizabeth never wanted to be Queen, biographers tell us; she is modest and unassuming in spite of her position. As a result, her subjects find it easier to relate to her and even feel sorry for her having to sacrifice herself for the nation. The Queen thinks of herself as an ordinary person and in some ways, lives quite simply. For instance, she drinks barley water and believes in natural remedies. She often drives herself from London to her weekend home at Windsor Castle rather than rely on a chauffeur. Like other Britons, she spends a lot of evenings eating her dinner from a tray in front of the television. She even carries an ordinary handbag, which she stows behind the throne during ceremonies.

Though she lives surrounded by cultural treasures, the Queen is not very interested in the arts or culture. She is said to be happiest when relaxing with her family or tramping around outdoors with her dogs and horses, dressed in headscarf and rubber boots. She finds time for this during her twenty weeks of vacation each year at her private estates of Balmoral and Sandringham, or in the Great Park at Windsor. Some of Elizabeth's eleven corgi dogs even travel with her on the royal plane and train. She is passionately devoted to her hobbies of horse racing and horse breeding, and has an entire library of technical books on these subjects. She enjoys riding, watching her horses run at British and European races, and visiting stud farms in America where her horses breed. This love of country life and animals endears the Queen to the British people, millions of whom share her enthusiasm.

Britain's Poet Laureate, Ted Hughes, has described the Queen as a "flawless mirror" of the national character. Many Britons read into the Queen's personality what they like to see in themselves. The British are known for hiding their emotions behind a wall of reserve and a "stiff upper lip." The Queen is famous for her dignified, serious expression in public, for being "calm in joy, calm in grief," for her "selfless" devotion to duty. She is brisk and efficient in her work life, as well as remarkably healthy and strong. Yet she is said to be funny and caring. For example, before posing for one of her many official portraits, she asked the painter, "Now then, with teeth or without?" She would seem to be a perfectly balanced individual for someone under so much pressure.

The Queen Wants a Raise

The Queen was highly respected and widely admired. But when she asked for a pay raise in 1970, she came under fire from politicians and the public for her privileged financial position, which was at the time tax-free. The controversy over the Civil List threatened both the popularity of the monarchy and of the Queen herself.

Parliament had not raised the Queen's annual allowance for her official duties since it was set at $855,000 in 1952. Prince Philip had long complained that this was not enough in spite of the Palace's efforts to economize. Parliament appointed a Select Committee to look into the matter when the Queen finally requested more money. Counsel for the prosecution was Member of Parliament (MP) Willie Hamilton, who became Britain's best-known anti-monarchist. He called the Queen's request "an arrogant display of insensitive greed."

The Tory Party, which was then in power under PM Edward Heath, was generally sympathetic to the Queen's case. The Labour and Liberal parties, however, proposed setting up a Department of the Crown to oversee royal finances and report to Parliament. In the end, a compromise was reached: the original Civil List amount was doubled to $1,764,000, with the amount to be reviewed every ten years.

Money, Monarchy, and Public Opinion

Never before had there been such an open inquiry into a monarch's finances or so much public discussion of how much the monarchy cost the nation. Usually people saved their anger for politicians; now, with the focus on money, some turned their resentment on the Queen. Why should she live in luxury and pay no taxes while ordinary Britons were struggling to pay their bills and keep their jobs? "I object to even one penny of my husband's hard-earned money contributing to making the world's richest woman richer," one taxpayer wrote to Hamilton.

The most commonly heard argument against the monarchy has always been its enormous expense. Yet it is the expensive trappings of monarchy that make the whole system worthwhile

---

Republicanism in Britain

Critics have been predicting an end to the monarchy since the democratic writings of Thomas Paine in the 1790's, but the only time such ideas took hold was in the 1860's, when Queen Victoria went into retirement after her husband's death. The people were unwilling to support a queen they never saw. Republican (pro-republic, anti-monarchy) organizations sprang up around the country, then faded after Victoria resumed her public life.

During the reign of Elizabeth II, public opinion polls have stayed constant at about 90 percent of Britons in favor of the monarchy and 10 percent in favor of a republic. Republican beliefs are most popular away from the centers of power, in the pro-Labour North of England as well as Scotland and Wales (parts of the United Kingdom which once had their own monarchs). The majority of Britons regard republicans as eccentrics or radicals. There is no real republican movement or serious debate about the monarchy today, according to out-spoken republican author Tom Nairn. For this he blames inertia (reluctance to change) and the Palace's power to stage grand events and control the press.

---

to most Britons. When asked why they favored keeping the monarchy, forty percent of those polled in 1969 gave "pomp and pageantry" as a reason. Such things cannot be pared down to be cheaper, explains court historian Hugh Montgomery-Massingberd. "Either one has a splendid show or one has nothing." Besides, supporters argue, it is a harmless show that the people like, so why not keep it? Monarchists also say that the Queen more than makes up for her expense by encouraging tourism and trade. And income to the government from the Crown Estates, which include farmland and business property all over the country, amounts to $122 million per year.

Toward the Silver Jubilee

In 1977, the Palace was planning the "splendid show" of the Queen's Silver Jubilee, celebrating her twenty-five years on the throne. Anti-monarchists charge that such events distract people from the real problems of the day. Britain's social and economic problems were certainly real enough in the 1970's. The country suffered from the world oil crisis, and inflation sent prices ever higher under both Conservative and Labour governments. There were national miners' strikes in 1972 and 1974 as trade unions gained influence. The "troubles" between Catholics and Protestants in Northern Ireland became more violent and bitter, touching the Queen personally when a terrorist bomb killed her husband's uncle, Lord Mountbatten.

The Queen wanted her Jubilee to be relatively simple and inexpensive out of respect for the growing numbers of unemployed Britons. But as the day grew near, the people became swept up in the spirit of the celebration. Thirty-two new books about the Queen were published. Londoners raised funds for six thousand street parties, while festivities in small towns ranged from barn dances to thanksgiving services.

In her most successful walkabout ever, the Queen strolled

through the throngs of people around St. Paul's Cathedral.
"We have come here because we love you!" someone shouted.
"I feel it and it means so much to me," replied the Queen.
After fireworks that night, huge crowds collected around
Buckingham Palace to salute the Queen in a party atmosphere
that reminded many of VE Day at the end of World War II.
The people of Britain had not elected their Queen, but with
their jubilation at her Jubilee, they gave her a strong vote of
confidence.

Making the most of her popularity during the Jubilee year,
the Queen was a tireless traveler. She covered seventy-one
hundred miles at home and thirty-seven thousand overseas,
attending eight hundred events held in her honor and shaking
an average of five thousand hands a day. The driving force
behind much of her travel was her commitment to the
Commonwealth.

Chapter 6

The Commonwealth "Family"

"One of the more encouraging developments since the war has been the birth of the Commonwealth," the Queen believes. Elizabeth has presided over and promoted the growth of this unusual association from a mere eight members in 1952 to thirty in 1970 to fifty today. Her efforts have helped keep the Commonwealth together through many conflicts.

The idea of a Commonwealth of nations rose from the ashes of the British Empire after the two world wars. Several former colonies had already been given self-governing status as Dominions and had fought with the Allies in World War I. With the organization of the Commonwealth, Britain could keep former colonies tied to itself and each other while gradually allowing them independence. In 1931, the Dominions of Australia, Canada, the Irish Free State, New Zealand, Newfoundland (later part of Canada), and South Africa were declared independent, free and equal members of the British Commonwealth, with their own parliaments and loyalty to the Crown.

It was not until the rapid "throwing away of empire" after World War II that the modern multiracial Commonwealth really took shape. India pointed the direction for the association when it finally won independence after years of violent struggle. One by one, nearly every British colony in Africa, Asia, the Caribbean, the Mediterranean, and the Pacific followed suit and joined the Commonwealth. The face of the organization was transformed from European-dominated and white to mainly nonwhite and multiracial.

In 1949, India became the first country to declare itself a republic (rather than a monarchy) while remaining in the Commonwealth. This meant a new role for the British monarch: hereafter he or she would be Head of the Commonwealth but not necessarily head of each state within it. Though some critics think the Commonwealth never found a role for itself in the world, the Queen pledged herself with zeal to her role as its head.

A Diverse "Family"

Today the Commonwealth—comprising one fourth of the world's population and one third of its states—is known for its remarkable diversity. Its members range from tiny island nations and some of the world's poorest countries to the large, wealthy nations of Australia and Canada. More than half of the member states of the Commonwealth have populations of under one million; many are developing countries that depend on others for aid.

A wide range of religions, languages, racial and ethnic groups, and political philosophies are represented in the Commonwealth. While sixteen of its countries are headed by the Queen, several have their own monarchs and twenty-nine are republics headed by presidents. Some Commonwealth countries have freely elected parliaments while others are military dictatorships.

Originally, the purpose of the Commonwealth was to promote British ideals of parliamentary democracy and tolerance, as well as economic cooperation. Joining the association was supposed to help colonies make the transition to independence. As the membership grew and Britain became less dominant, Commonwealth interests broadened. Since 1971, it has declared its commitment to principles such as world peace, racial equality, fair trade, and economic justice.

THE COMMONWEALTH FAMILY
One Fourth of the World

The multiracial Commonwealth "family" now consists of fifty independent states with one fourth of the world's population (1.4 billion people). There are member countries on every continent and in every ocean. They represent a variety of political systems, but all recognize the Queen as Head of the Commonwealth. Commonwealth leaders exchange information and cooperate on scientific and technical projects through their headquarters in London, biennial conferences, and numerous voluntary organizations.

Country	Date Joined	Status
Antiqua and Barbuda	1981	Queen Head of State
Australia	1931	Queen Head of State
Bahamas	1973	Queen Head of State
Bangladesh	1972	Republic
Barbados	1966	Queen Head of State
Belize	1981	Queen Head of State
Botswana	1966	Republic
Britain	founder	Queen Head of State
Brunei	1984	Has own monarch
Canada	1931	Queen Head of State
Cyprus	1961	Republic
Dominica	1978	Republic
The Gambia	1965	Republic
Ghana	1957	Republic

Country	Date Joined	Status
Grenada	1974	Queen Head of State
Guyana	1966	Republic
India	1947	Republic
Jamaica	1962	Queen Head of State
Kenya	1963	Republic
Kiribati	1979	Republic
Lesotho	1966	Has own monarch
Malawi	1964	Republic
Malaysia	1957	Has own monarch
Maldives	1982	Republic
Malta	1964	Republic
Mauritius	1968	Republic
Namibia	1990	Republic
Nauru	1968	Republic
New Zealand	1931	Queen Head of State
Nigeria	1960	Republic
Pakistan	1989	Republic
Papua New Guinea	1975	Queen Head of State
St. Christopher-Nevis	1983	Queen Head of State
St. Lucia	1979	Queen Head of State
St. Vincent and the Grenadines	1979	Queen Head of State
Seychelles	1976	Republic
Sierra Leone	1961	Republic
Singapore	1965	Republic

Country	Date Joined	Status
Solomon Islands	1978	Queen Head of State
Sri Lanka (formerly Ceylon)	1948	Republic
Swaziland	1968	Has own monarch
Tanzania	1961	Republic
Tonga	1970	Has own monarch
Trinidad and Tobago	1962	Republic
Tuvalu	1978	Queen Head of State
Uganda	1962	Republic
Vanuatu	1980	Republic
Western Samoa	1970	Republic
Zambia	1964	Republic
Zimbabwe (formerly Rhodesia)	1980	Republic

Source: The Commonwealth Institute, London, 1992

The Queen speaks of the Commonwealth members as a "family," implying that they are on friendly terms and share certain values and experiences. As a group, most Commonwealth countries get along reasonably well with each other. But India and Pakistan went to war against each other twice and Pakistan, like South Africa, Burma, and Ireland, eventually left the "club" due to conflicts. (Pakistan rejoined in 1989.) Other states remain members in spite of strong disagreements with fellow members.

What holds this loosely organized "family" together? All the members share historical ties to the British Crown. Most have been influenced by British institutions: the English language, educational system (which trained many Commonwealth leaders), and Parliament—not to mention the game of cricket. Some states, such as New Zealand, are full of people with British relatives or ancestors. The people in the Commonwealth also come together through various professional and civic organizations, training programs, cultural exchanges, and sporting events. Perhaps the most visible link between members of the Commonwealth "family" is the Queen.

The Queen's Commitment to the Commonwealth

"I want to show that the crown is not merely an abstract symbol of our unity," declared the Queen in 1954 in New Zealand, "but a personal and living bond between you and me." Though some question the loyalty that inhabitants of the Commonwealth feel for the Queen today, no one doubts the sincerity of her dedication to Commonwealth peace and unity.

Ever since delivering more than one hundred speeches on her first Commonwealth tour in 1953-1954, the Queen has devoted much of her time to Commonwealth affairs. She is said to know more about the Commonwealth than any of her government ministers. This is due to her years of travel throughout the member countries, her faithful attendance at Commonwealth Conferences, and her warm friendships with Commonwealth leaders. Elizabeth has known many senior statesmen since her youth and has drawn on those friendships to win trust and spur cooperation among the association's members.

Just as she has special access to Commonwealth leaders, the Queen has tried to make herself accessible to the people of the Commonwealth. The first walkabout, as we have seen, took place in New Zealand. The Queen's Christmas Speech is broadcast to the entire Commonwealth and usually contains a message of international appeal. She has learned many national anthems and native dances as a gesture of respect for the countries she visits, and she takes obvious pleasure in her Commonwealth tours. According to one journalist, "She is never so happy as when she is being welcomed by a crowd of tribal dancers in grass skirts."

The Queen has often made Commonwealth appearances against the advice of her government. For instance, she went ahead with a trip to Ghana in 1961 at a time of civil war because she felt that without her show of support, the Commonwealth might lose its oldest African member. As it turned out, the Queen survived a torch-lit procession in an open car with President Nkrumah, and Ghana stayed in the club. She likewise showed courage in traveling to Quebec, Canada, in 1964 when angry French-Canadians were pushing for an independent Quebec, and in attending a crucial Commonwealth Conference in Africa at the height of civil war in Rhodesia.

Challenges to the Commonwealth

The Commonwealth has weathered a number of crises during the Queen's reign. Many have focused on Africa, where "winds of change" (in the words of PM Macmillan) were sweeping European influence out and black African nationalism in.

In 1949, South Africa's Nationalist-Afrikaner party began a policy of apartheid (separation of white and nonwhite people). This sort of discrimination went against the spirit of tolerance that the Commonwealth represented. Increasingly, African and Asian members demanded that South Africa leave the club. It finally did so in 1961.

Britain, however, maintained its tradition of trade with South Africa well into the 1980's and refused to join the Commonwealth's call for sanctions (a ban on trade to force South Africa to change its policies). Disagreements about sanctions drove a wedge between Britain and other Commonwealth members, as well as between the Queen (who championed the Commonwealth view) and PM Margaret Thatcher.

A second area of conflict was the British decision to join the European Economic Community (EEC) in 1973. This seemed like a betrayal to Commonwealth leaders, who felt they had not been consulted. They were also upset about the loss of their trade advantages with Britain; now they would have to pay taxes on their exports.

By casting its lot with European unity and cooperation, Britain signaled a shift in international loyalties. It saw its economic interests lying closer to home rather than across the seas it once had ruled. Would this mean the breakup of the Commonwealth "family"? "The new links with Europe will not replace those with the Commonwealth," the Queen said in her 1972 Christmas Speech. "They cannot alter our historical and personal attachments with kinsmen and friends overseas." Nevertheless those bonds were loosening.

Behind the Scenes at Lusaka

Has the Queen's commitment to the Commonwealth really made a difference in people's lives? Perhaps not, except for her presence at Lusaka, Zambia in 1979—one of the few politically important moments in the Queen's reign. Here she showed how a royal style of low-key statesmanship behind the scenes could change the course of events.

The occasion was a Commonwealth Conference, the issue at hand the future of Rhodesia. In 1965, the white government of Ian Smith had made its own unilateral (one-sided) declaration of independence. Britain would not recognize this independence until its last African colony drew up a plan for rule by Rhodesia's black majority. Britain stopped trade with Rhodesia, but this did not result in a change in policy. Civil

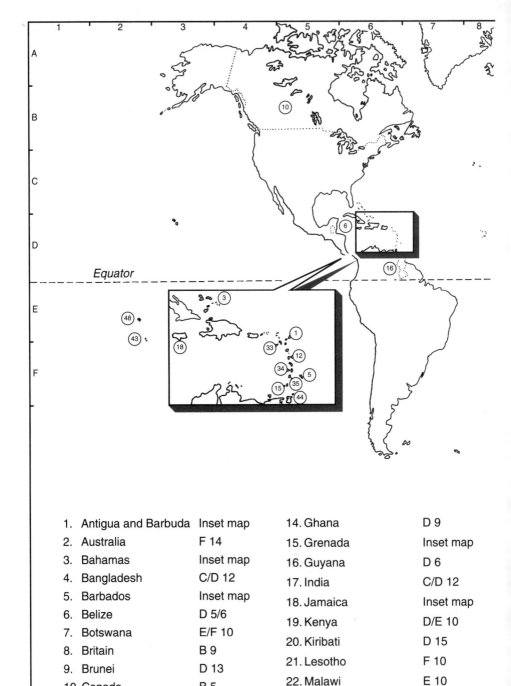

1.	Antigua and Barbuda	Inset map	
2.	Australia	F 14	
3.	Bahamas	Inset map	
4.	Bangladesh	C/D 12	
5.	Barbados	Inset map	
6.	Belize	D 5/6	
7.	Botswana	E/F 10	
8.	Britain	B 9	
9.	Brunei	D 13	
10.	Canada	B 5	
11.	Cyprus	C 10	
12.	Dominica	Inset map	
13.	The Gambia	D 8	
14.	Ghana	D 9	
15.	Grenada	Inset map	
16.	Guyana	D 6	
17.	India	C/D 12	
18.	Jamaica	Inset map	
19.	Kenya	D/E 10	
20.	Kiribati	D 15	
21.	Lesotho	F 10	
22.	Malawi	E 10	
23.	Malaysia	D 13	
24.	Maldives	D 11	
25.	Malta	C 9	

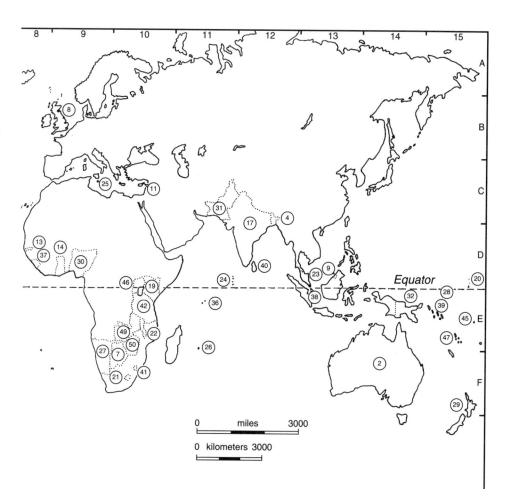

26. Mauritius	E 11	38. Singapore	D/E 13
27. Namibia	E/F 9	39. Solomon Islands	E 15
28. Nauru	D/E 15	40. Sri Lanka	D 12
29. New Zealand	F 15	41. Swaziland	F 10
30. Nigeria	D 9	42. Tanzania	E 10
31. Pakistan	C 11	43. Tonga	E/F 2
32. Papua New Guinea	E 14	44. Trinidad and Tobago	Inset Map
33. St Christopher-Nevis	Inset Map	45. Tuvalu	E 15
34. St Lucia	Inset Map	46. Uganda	D/E 10
35. St Vincent	Inset Map	47. Vanuatu	E 15
& the Grenadines		48. Western Samoa	E 2
36. Seychelles	E 11	49. Zambia	E 10
37. Sierra Leone	D 8	50. Zimbabwe	E 10

war broke out between Smith's government and black nationalist parties. The conflict reached a peak in 1979 with a Smith-backed black bishop heading the government, a breakdown in talks between Rhodesia and Britain, and African members threatening to quit the Commonwealth unless there was a speedy settlement. They feared that Conservative PM Thatcher would not make a fair deal for the country's blacks.

The Queen stepped into this crisis with the goal of keeping the various parties talking so that a solution could be reached. She arrived early for the conference in Lusaka and visited with her old friends President Kaunda of Zambia and President Nyerere of Tanzania. She stayed away from official conference meetings but continued to act as a "referee," pleading with both African and British leaders for compromise. The Queen brought a "healing touch" to the tense situation, in the view of then-Commonwealth Secretary-General Ramphal. There were further talks in London, a ceasefire in the civil war, independence, and free elections for what became black-ruled Zimbabwe in 1980. The Queen could take credit for paving the way for this successful outcome.

The Future of the Commonwealth

Not all Britons share the Queen's enthusiasm for the Commonwealth. "She may take pride in the Commonwealth, but her people for the most part, don't," according to the *Spectator*, "and regard her love for this hybrid offspring of the empire with deepening distaste."

One reason for this feeling is resentment against the large numbers of Asian and Caribbean immigrants, who have drastically changed the makeup of British society in recent years. When the Queen made a Christmas speech in 1983 about how the Commonwealth could help bridge the gap between rich and poor countries, she was criticized for caring too much about the Commonwealth and too little about the concerns of ordinary Britons. Some politicians see her attachment to the Commonwealth as looking backward, and think she should be giving more attention to Britain's future role in Europe.

Is the Commonwealth just a sentimental holdover from the days of empire which has lost whatever purpose it had? It is no longer a vital trade alliance or a symbol of British-style parliamentary government. It lacks the power and prestige of the United Nations. But as the world's only free association of multiracial states, it stands committed to racial and economic equality. It is, as one journalist suggests, "a unique experiment in human relations." And it is still useful as a friendly forum for discussion and argument among diverse states, according to one recent study.

The Queen's deep belief in the value of the Commonwealth has never wavered. It is part of her legacy. It is an institution that stands for certain ideals in a changing world—much like the monarchy. Whatever the final judgment is on the history and fate of the Commonwealth, it will also be a judgment on the Queen and her loyalty to this large, often unruly "family."

The Queen has shown a similar loyalty to a very different family that has also had its share of joys and troubles in the past decade—the Royal Family.

Chapter 7

The Royal Family

"Royalty puts a human face on the operations of government," the Archbishop of Canterbury said in 1980. If anything shows the humanity of royalty, it is their family life. They go through the same stages of growth, the same ups and downs as other families. The difference is that the Royal Family is always on public display and is expected to be a model for the nation's families.

The current Royal Family is the most heavily publicized of any in history. This is due to its size, to the importance accorded the family by the Queen, and to the Palace's stress on family in its public relations. The Queen has four children, an outspoken husband, an independent sister, and a beloved mother who was queen before her. Elizabeth cultivated her family as a team that could share the increasing workload of public engagements, and appeal to a wide range of people. As the Queen entered middle age and her children grew up, attention turned away from Elizabeth and became riveted on the younger members of the Royal Family.

The model family proved that it was all too human when Princess Margaret, the Queen's sister, divorced in 1978. The shadow of divorce was to haunt the family again later. But first came their moment of glory with the wedding of Prince Charles in 1981.

A Royal Wedding

The Prince of Wales, age thirty-two, had been known as "the world's most eligible bachelor" for several years. He was not only heir to the throne but handsome, athletic, funny, and intelligent. He was the first royal to complete a college degree, receiving honors in history at Cambridge University. His hobbies ranged from polo to gardening, his interests from architecture to ecology.

For his bride, Charles chose Lady Diana Spencer, a nineteen-year-old nursery school teacher. She was a commoner (that is, not a royal), but she came from an aristocratic family that was well known at the palace. At first overwhelmed by publicity, "Shy Di" soon came to shine in the media with her good looks, poise, and fresh view of royal life.

A public holiday was declared for the royal wedding on July 29, 1981. Three quarters of a billion people watched the ceremony on television. When the newlyweds appeared on the balcony of Buckingham Palace, the crowd yelled, "Kiss her!" and the couple obliged. The kiss and the interviews they granted the press seemed to mark a new era of modernity and openness at the palace.

The Diana Decade

So began a decade of media obsession with the Prince and Princess of Wales, especially with Diana. Photographers followed her everywhere, even to the corner candy store and to private beaches during her pregnancy. The publicity became so intense that the Queen was moved to intervene. At an informal meeting with the heads of the major British media, she asked them to stop harassing her daughter-in-law.

The press and the public seemed irresistibly drawn to Diana even more than they had been to the young Queen. Diana's photo sold newspapers; her dresses had the fashion industry scrambling for imitations. She was praised for her devoted attention to her children, William, born in 1982, and Harry, born in 1984, whom she brought with her on royal tours. Prince Charles seemed to be forgotten in the frenzy; even the Queen seemed less popular now by contrast.

The newlywed Prince Andrew, Duke of York, and his bride, the former Sarah Ferguson, leaving Westminster Abbey. (AP/Wide World Photos)

The Other Royals

Who are the other members of the Royal Family? They are "a very ordinary family for whom extraordinary claims are made by its supporters," grumbles anti-monarchist Hamilton. Perhaps their position and fame leads the public to have unusual expectations of them.

One who has definitely felt the pressure to distinguish herself is Princess Anne, the Queen's daughter. In her youth, she was a prizewinning horseback rider and even joined the Olympic team. Since 1970, she has been best known for her charity work and worldwide travels on behalf of the Save the Children Fund. Anne married an officer and fellow horseman, Mark Phillips, in 1973. But like her aunt Margaret, she has protected her children from the media and royal obligations. Apparently she does not want them to grow up as she did.

Prince Andrew won public affection when he served as a helicopter pilot during the Falklands War in 1982. His wedding to the fun-loving Sarah Ferguson ("Fergie"), another commoner, was watched by millions in 1986.

Prince Edward has yet to make his mark. He has spent time playing rugby, serving in the Marines, and dabbling in theater.

The Duke of Edinburgh has tried to be his own man rather than merely the husband of the Queen. While the Queen must be neutral, Philip never hesitates to express his opinion— sometimes to the horror of the Palace. He has an irreverent sense of humor and even collects cartoons about the Royal Family. He has used his keen interest in technology to modernize business procedures at the palace.

Some say that of all the Royal Family, the Queen Mother is the most popular. Unlike her daughter, she smiles warmly for the camera and is never shy with the crowds. Her many fans turned out for a parade in honor of her ninetieth birthday in 1990.

The Work of the Royals

Together members of the Royal Family take part in thousands of public engagements and serve as heads of hundreds of charitable groups. They represent the Queen in more places than she alone could go, as when Prince Charles visited British troops in Saudi Arabia during the Gulf War in

1991. Like the Queen, they are goodwill ambassadors.

Family members receive large allowances from the government for their work. In 1992, these totaled $2.8 million, ranging from $152,000 for Prince Edward to $972,000 for the Queen Mother. In November of 1992, however, the Queen announced that henceforth she will pay the expenses of five family members whose 1992 allowances amounted to $1.3 million, roughly half of the 1992 total for family members. (The Prince and Princess of Wales live on the income from lands in the Duchy of Cornwall, one quarter of which they pay back to the state.)

Some Britons have been angered over the years by the cost of supporting the royals, while others say that the family is hardworking. Princess Anne is especially admired for her diligence. In 1990, for example, she had 449 official engagements in Britain and 319 overseas, compared to the Queen's 476 at home and 94 abroad.

Why is it important for the royals to appear at so many public functions? Their presence often boosts morale. Whether chatting with the forgotten residents of an old-folks home or speaking at the annual meeting of an organization, attention from the royals motivates people. The royal stamp of approval helps raise money for many good causes. It can also influence public opinion on social issues of the day. For instance, the Queen's shaking hands with a leprosy patient in the 1950's and Princess Diana hugging young victims of AIDS in the 1980's helped combat prejudice against those feared diseases.

The Queen and the "Iron Lady"

The Queen continued to spread goodwill on her overseas tours as she traveled to the Middle East and China for the first time in the 1980's. She also visited long-term friends of Britain such as India and the United States, braving thunderstorms to stay at President Reagan's California ranch.

But the 1980's were hardly a time of goodwill in the British political arena. The country was split over the ultra-conservative policies of Margaret Thatcher, the country's first woman Prime Minister. Thatcher lost no time in tackling rising prices and clamping down on workers' strikes. She transferred

Margaret Thatcher, Prime Minister from 1979 to 1990; the Queen's relations with her were strained. (AP/Wide World Photos)

many nationalized industries to private hands and cut back drastically on public services such as health care. The number of unemployed people rose to three million by the mid-1980's, evoking the hard times of the 1930's. Nevertheless, the "Iron Lady" was reelected twice by large majorities. She was respected for her strong stand against Argentina in the war over the faraway Falkland Islands, and for bringing prosperity to parts of Britain.

The Queen was reportedly dismayed with Thatcher's hard-line approach to government at home and to Commonwealth issues like South African sanctions. Some sources say the Queen was also irritated by Thatcher's tendency to act like a head of state, as in arriving at the scene of national disasters before the Queen. She even upstaged the Queen by wearing a royal favorite shade of blue.

Though "Shy Di" and the "Iron Lady" grabbed the head-lines in the 1980's, the Queen was secure in her popularity. There had been general alarm in 1981 when a bystander fired blank shots at the Queen during her birthday parade, and again in 1982 when a stranger broke into the Queen's bedroom at Buckingham Palace. The press and the public were outraged that anyone would dare attack the Queen, whom the *Times* had once called "the inner spiritual essence of our national life."

Money and Family Problems

It has often been said that the Queen's greatest problems arose from her paying no taxes and from the behavior of some members of the Royal Family. In 1990, the government imposed a highly unpopular poll tax on everyone in the land, including the poor and elderly. Of course, the Queen did not have to pay, in spite of her enormous wealth (estimated at between $1.5 billion and $10 billion). In a *Times* survey, three out of four Britons said they thought the Queen should pay taxes like other people.

In November of 1992, fire destroyed a section of Windsor Castle. Who would foot the repair bill? (The cost of restoration is expected to range between $60 million and $90 million.) Many people expressed outrage at the prospect of covering this expense at a time when one in ten Britons was out of work and the country was in the midst of its most prolonged economic slump since the 1930's. The same month, the government announced that in 1993 the Queen would begin paying income tax as well as some of the allowances to members of the Royal Family. This surprising announcement was widely interpreted as a well-timed public relations gesture intended to bolster support for the monarchy.

Perhaps even more damaging to the reputation of the monarchy were the highly publicized marriage problems of the younger royals. Exposed to the relentless glare of press and television coverage, their conduct seemed to many to tarnish the mystique on which the continuation of the monarchy depends. In 1992, Princess Anne and her husband were divorced after three years of separation; later in the year she married Timothy J. H. Laurence, a naval officer, marking the first time that the son or daughter of a British monarch remarried after divorce. In March of 1992, after several years of lurid press coverage and speculation about the state of their marriage, Fergie and Prince Andrew announced their separation; in August of the same year, British tabloids (heavily illustrated newspapers that specialize in sensationalistic stories) featured photographs of Fergie, topless, with an American suitor in St. Tropez, France.

The most intense press coverage of the royals in 1992 focused on the Prince and Princess of Wales. Their marriage had long been rumored to be unhappy, but the 1992 publication of a best-selling book sympathetic to Diana, portraying her as a tormented soul, revealed the conflicts between Charles and Diana in unprecedented detail. In

93

December of 1992, their formal separation was announced. While PM John Major assured Parliament and the British people that the succession to the throne would not be affected by the separation, anti-monarchists pointed to the instability of the situation as further evidence that the monarchy has outlived its time.

Amazingly, the Queen's image has remained untouched by all the scandal. Her personal behavior is still beyond reproach. It is the younger royals who "don't know how to behave," a majority of Britons agreed in a 1992 opinion poll. Many wondered if the Queen was referring to the Royal Family during her historic first speech to the European Parliament the same year. "The European family contains diverse personalities," she said. "In this, and in its need for tolerance and mutual support, it is like any family."

In a speech after the Windsor Castle fire, the Queen conceded that 1992 had been a "horrible year." Luckily for the Palace, 1992 was also the anniversary of the Queen's fortieth year on the throne. It was the occasion for another television program that would show how hard the Queen was working for her country.

Princess Elizabeth at the wheel of an ambulance, in training as an Auxiliary Transport Service officer in 1945. (AP/Wide World Photos)

Chapter 8

Legacy

To make the latest documentary about the Queen, another hand-picked BBC team spent a year filming her at work. The film was called *Elizabeth R*, after the Queen's official signature (*R* is for Regina, a Latin term for Queen). It showed the Queen practicing a speech, having her weekly chat with the Prime Minister, attending a Commonwealth Conference, and joking with Congress on a tour of the United States. There were also informal glimpses of her sitting for a portrait and cheering on her racehorses. The overall impression was that of a dignified monarch who was still very much in command.

It was important for the Palace to convey this message at this time. The Queen was sixty-five, the age most people retire. She was visibly tired and traveled less, but showed no signs of giving up her office. In her Christmas Speech the year before, she had said, "I feel the same obligation to you that I felt in 1952. With your prayers, and your help, and with the love and support of my family, I shall try to serve you in the years to come." This disappointed some Britons, who felt the Queen should step down and make way for her urbane son, Charles, as king. Others saw the Queen's determination as yet another sign of her devotion to duty—for traditionally, British monarchs rule until their death.

The Queen's Influence

Of the thirty-nine English monarchs before her in the past thousand years, only five have ruled as long as the Queen. She is now the most experienced statesman in the world, according to her biographers. She has certainly witnessed dramatic changes over forty years, just as she has known and worked with many Prime Ministers and world leaders. But unlike other statesmen, she has never been responsible for making decisions or taking action. Her style has been to set a tone or example by her royal presence in order to cement relationships. If she has made a mark on political history, it is in her efforts to strengthen the Commonwealth and to resolve the 1979 Rhodesia crisis. In this way, she has helped to shape and stabilize the post-World War II international order.

"There isn't any power," Prince Charles wrote of the monarch's role in his autobiography. "But there can be influence. The influence is in direct proportion to the respect that people have for you." Given the Queen's great popularity, it seems likely that her occasional word in a politician's ear may have had an impact on events in Britain, too. But this is a sensitive area. We may never know the extent of the Queen's influence because of her government's practice of keeping many documents secret for thirty, fifty, or one hundred years—or forever.

What we do know is that the Queen made herself into Britain's most valuable export with her frequent travels and walkabouts. This has meant increased trade possibilities and an enhanced international image for Britain. Likewise, ever since forty thousand Americans traveled to London to see her Coronation, the Queen, her family, and their royal ceremonies have stimulated tourism. This, too, has brought both money and prestige to the country.

"The Majesty of the Common Man"

The Queen's main duty, and perhaps her crowning achievement, has been to keep the British monarchy alive in an increasingly democratic age. She has done this, as we have seen, by becoming a modern, popular ruler, maintaining the magic of monarchy while making herself accessible to the people.

Her Majesty Queen Elizabeth II represents "the majesty of the common man," suggests biographer Robert Lacey. In this, she follows in the steps of her father and grandfather. She has shown that a monarch, while a powerful symbol, can be a rather ordinary person fulfilling an extraordinary role. She has stood for middle-class values of hard work, family, and devotion to duty in spite of her great wealth and position. This won the hearts of her countrymen. Whatever their feelings about the monarchy, they seem to admire the Queen personally for her life of service and sacrifice.

Is respect and affection for the Queen truly the bond that holds the nation together? That depends on how well-matched she is to her people, says historian Anthony Jay. She can unite Britons "only so long as people see her, know what she stands for (and will not stand for), identify with her, and believe that her behavior and her values correspond with their own." Miraculously, through all the changes since 1952, the Queen has kept the people's trust. She has managed to be seen both as an inspirational ideal and as someone "just like us." Carefully performing her role, attuned to her audience, she has done her best to preserve faith in the monarchy.

The Future of the Monarchy

The Queen has always said she would step down if the people decided they did not want a monarchy. This is unlikely so long as she is on the throne. But what of the future? The Queen's stellar performance will be a hard act to follow. Can any heir to the throne from the postwar generation be such an example to the nation? Can the institution outlive the Queen's personal popularity?

The seeds of the collapse of the monarchy may have already been sown during Elizabeth's reign. It is hard for any ideal to survive the questioning spirit and flexible morality of the late twentieth century. The monarchy's image has been hurt by

In Line for the Throne

According to the laws of accession, heirs to the throne must be Protestant descendants of the granddaughter of King James I (the king who united the kingdoms of England, Scotland, and Ireland in 1603). Male heirs are first in line in order of their birth; thus, the Queen's sons, Charles, Andrew, and Edward, precede her daughter, Anne. Traditionally, British monarchs do not retire but pass on their title immediately upon their death to their heir. A dead monarch's wife or husband cannot inherit the throne but does remain a member of the Royal Family.

As of 1990, the first ten people in line for the throne after Queen Elizabeth II were her children and grandchildren, followed by Princess Margaret and her children, and more distant relatives:

1. *The Prince of Wales (Charles)*
2. *Prince William of Wales (Charles' son)*
3. *Prince Henry of Wales (Charles' son)*
4. *The Duke of York (Andrew)*
5. *Princess Beatrice (Andrew's daughter)*
6. *Princess Eugenie (Andrew's daughter)*
7. *Prince Edward*
8. *The Princess Royal (Anne)*
9. *Peter Phillips (Anne's son)*
10. *Zara Phillips (Anne's daughter)*

investigations of the Queen's finances and scandals within the Royal Family. With some of the secrecy removed, it no longer seems so perfect and untouchable an institution. Many people are freer now with their criticisms. Fewer and fewer Britons (69 percent in 1990, 46 percent in 1992) expect the system to be around in fifty years, according to recent national polls. They apparently do not trust any heir to the throne to carry off the role properly.

Britain is also a very different place in 1992 than it was in 1952. It has become a diverse, multiracial society that is increasingly tied to the European Community. Some people ask if it is still appropriate for the Queen to head the Church of England when so many other religions now abound in Britain. Others wonder whether the EC will require new citizen's rights that alter the relationship between British "subjects" and their monarch. These and other new conditions may make the country less receptive to monarchy in the next century.

But royal historian Philip Ziegler insists there will always be a king or queen in Britain. He believes that the monarchy appeals to both the conservatism and the romanticism of the British people. They shudder at the thought of the alternatives to monarchy. Electing a president seems too "vulgar," risky, and changeable. Adopting the Dutch or Scandinavian model, in which kings and queens have only ceremonial duties and live modestly, is also unthinkable to many. As long as the Queen is on the throne, writes biographer Anne Morrow, "there is a comforting, warm, secure feeling, even if the monarchy is a bit old-fashioned."

Clearly, most British people are attached to the "splendid show" and link to the past that the monarchy offers. Loyalty to the Crown is woven into the fabric of their lives: it is taught in their schools, inscribed in their military certificates, invoked in their courts and churches. Britons participate in the system of monarchy and endorse its prestige—even if they have doubts

Rising above controversy and scandal, Queen Elizabeth II retains the love and respect of her people. (AP/Wide World Photos)

about it—every time they or someone they know accepts an honorary title, attends a palace garden party, or conducts business with a royal society. The monarchy's influence even thrives while the nation is asleep. One third of all Britons dream about the Queen, especially about being invited to tea, according to a recent book on the subject.

Wedded to Britain

In 1952, Elizabeth was a young wife and mother hoping to lead a "normal life." But from the moment she received the royal ring, she became wedded to her country, tied to her role. As Queen, she firmly stamped her signature on her office. Today, in the eyes of her people, she is the essence of what a modern queen should be; they can imagine no other.

How much longer will she reign? Will Queen Elizabeth II be the last British monarch, or will she be followed by one of her heirs? No one can predict these things. Whatever happens, Elizabeth's reputation is secure. She will be remembered for breathing life—her whole life—into an ancient symbol of national pride.

The Queen's Roles

As Head of State of Britain and fifteen other countries, as well as Head of the Commonwealth, the Queen fulfills many different roles. What exactly do these roles require her to do? Here are some examples:

"Fountain of Honor": Confers knighthoods and other honorary titles on more than three thousand people per year. E.g. in 1983 presented an Order of Merit to Mother Teresa for her lifelong devotion to the poor people of India.

"Fountain of Justice": Appoints judges, grants pardons to criminals, courts conducted in her name. E.g. in 1944 signed her first pardon while serving as counsellor of state to her father, King George VI.

Head of the Commonwealth: Visits Commonwealth countries, meets with their leaders, attends conferences, gives televised Christmas Speech. E.g. in 1961 visited president of Ghana as show of support in spite of terrorist threats; in 1979 met with leaders at Lusaka conference to pave way for an independent, black-ruled Rhodesia (Zimbabwe).

Head of State (Executive): Concludes treaties, represents Britain on official state visits abroad, receives foreign ambassadors and heads of state, visits British institutions, appears at national celebrations and disasters, presides at numerous ceremonies. E.g. in 1957 made first tour to United States; in 1966 visited site of Aberfan coal mine collapse in Wales; in 1990 hosted palace banquet for Polish President Lech Walesa; in 1992 made first speech to European Parliament in Strasbourg.

Head of State (Legislative): Summons and dismisses Parliament, approves all bills passed by Parliament, chooses Prime Minister (whoever is leader of majority party), consults weekly with Prime Minister, "advises and warns" government. E.g. in 1963 summoned A. D. Home as Prime Minister; in 1986 suggested that Thatcher's government do more to fight AIDS, resulting in a Cabinet committee on the question; in 1992 officially opened new Parliament under PM John Major with reading of Queen's Speech.

Supreme Governor of the Church of England, "Defender of the Faith": Opens general synod (meeting) of the Church of England, appoints top religious leaders, attends important religious ceremonies. E.g. annually gives out specially minted Maundy money to the elderly at Maundy Service before Easter; leads worship on Armistice Day.

Supreme Commander of the Armed Forces: Declares war, reviews troops at military bases and academies, awards military ranks and honors. E.g. in 1991 made special television speech to pray for safety of British soldiers in the Gulf War.

Time Line

1926	*April 21.* Princess Elizabeth Alexandra Mary born in London to Duke and Duchess of York.
1930	Elizabeth's sister, Princess Margaret Rose, born.
1931	Six dominions declared free and equal as first members of British Commonwealth.
1936	*"Year of Three Kings."* George V (Elizabeth's grandfather) dies; Edward VIII succeeds to throne, then abdicates; George VI (Elizabeth's father) becomes king.
1939	Meets Prince Philip of Greece, then a naval cadet.
	Britain declares war on Germany.
1944	Joins Auxiliary Territorial Service to help with war effort.
1945	*VE Day.* World War II is over.
1947	Coming-of-age speech in South Africa.
	November 20. Marries Prince Philip.
	India becomes independent, joins Commonwealth.
1948	Gives birth to Prince Charles.
1950	Gives birth to Princess Anne.
1952	*February 6.* King George VI dies, Elizabeth II becomes Queen.
1953	*June 2.* Queen's Coronation watched by millions on television.
1953-1954	Six-month Commonwealth tour.
1953-1955	Controversy over Princess Margaret's wish to marry a divorced man.
1957	Summons Macmillan as Prime Minister.
	Criticism of Queen in press.
1960	Gives birth to Prince Andrew.
	Princess Margaret marries Anthony Armstrong-Jones.
1961	South Africa leaves Commonwealth.
1963	Summons Home as Prime Minister.
1964	Gives birth to Prince Edward.

1969	Television documentary *Royal Family* shows the private lives of the royals for the first time.
	Investiture of Charles as Prince of Wales.
1970	First walkabout in New Zealand.
1971	Controversy over raising amount in Civil List (Queen's allowance).
1973	Britain enters the European Economic Community.
	Princess Anne marries Captain Mark Phillips.
1977	Silver Jubilee celebration for twenty-five years on the throne.
1978	Princess Margaret divorces.
1979	Referees conflict over Rhodesia at Lusaka conference, paving way for independence and black rule.
	Prime Minister Margaret Thatcher elected to first of three terms.
1981	Prince Charles marries Lady Diana Spencer.
	Start of "Diana Decade" (intense public interest in Princess of Wales).
	Blank shots fired at Queen during birthday parade.
1982	Britain defeats Argentina in Falklands War.
	Intruder arrested in Queen's bedroom.
	Princess of Wales gives birth to Prince William.
1986	Prince Andrew marries Sarah Ferguson.
1991	Britain takes part in Gulf War.
1992	Makes first speech to European Parliament.
	Princess Anne is divorced and, later in the year, remarries.
	Prince Andrew announces separation.
	Television documentary *Elizabeth R* commemorates forty years on the throne.
	Fire at Windsor Castle.
	Government announces that the Queen will pay income tax beginning in 1993 and will cover some of the Civil List allowances for members of the Royal Family.
	The Prince and Princess of Wales announce their separation.

Glossary

Abdicate: To give up the throne.

Accession: The act of coming into office as a king or queen.

Britain: Officially, the United Kingdom of Great Britain and Northern Ireland, comprising England, Scotland, Wales, and Northern Ireland.

British Empire: A group of colonies and territories around the world which were ruled by Britain between the seventeenth century and the mid-twentieth century.

Cabinet: A council of top government ministers who advise the Prime Minister.

Civil List: An allowance given by the government to the Queen to support her staff and official duties.

Commonwealth: A free association of fifty countries, most of them former British colonies, which promotes peace and racial tolerance; headed by the Queen.

Constitutional monarchy: A system of government headed by a king or queen whose powers are limited by the constitution.

Coronation: A formal ceremony of crowning a king or queen.

European Economic Community (now the European Community, or EC): An association of twelve European countries which promotes trade, cooperation, and unity.

Investiture: Official installation in an office or honorary title.

Monarch: A king or queen who reigns over a kingdom.

Monarchy: A system of government headed by a monarch who inherits the throne.

Parliament: A representative lawmaking body; in Britain, consisting of the elected House of Commons and the nonelected House of Lords.

Republic: A system of government headed by a president who is usually elected to represent the will of the people.

Royal prerogative: The Queen's privilege to exercise certain rights or choices, as in choosing a Prime Minister.

Tory: A member of the Conservative Party.

Walkabout: A public engagement where the Queen mingles freely with the crowd rather than being separated from them.

Bibliography

Cannon, John, and Ralph Griffiths. *The Oxford Illustrated History of the British Monarchy.* New York: Oxford University Press, 1988. An excellent source on the development of the monarchy, including one hundred pages on the monarchy since Queen Victoria.

Commonwealth Resource Centre. *The Commonwealth: What Is It?* London: Commonwealth Institute, 1992. A pamphlet that provides useful facts on the formation and function of the Commonwealth.

Hamilton, Alan. *Queen Elizabeth II.* London: Hamish Hamilton, 1982. Intended for young readers, this volume in the Profiles series offers an account of the Queen's life with a focus on her early years. Provides clear explanations of the Queen's duties but no historical background; illustrated with drawings rather than photos.

Hitchens, Christopher. "Windsor Knot: Is Britain Loosening the Royal Ties?" *The New York Times Magazine,* May 12, 1991. A critical observer examines tensions and signs of change within the monarchy and the Royal Family.

Lacey, Robert. *Majesty: Elizabeth II and the House of Windsor.* New York: Harcourt Brace Jovanovich, 1977. An important biography of the Queen, with vivid descriptions of her daily routine that will interest teenage readers. This balanced account of the first twenty-five years of Elizabeth's reign shows how she followed the example set by her father and grandfather.

Montgomery-Massingberd, Hugh. *Her Majesty the Queen.* London: William Collins' Sons, 1985. A handsomely produced coffee-table book that tells the story of the Queen's life and reign through classic photos. The text, more balanced than is typical of books of this kind, is also worth reading.

Morrow, Ann. *The Queen.* London: Granada, 1983. A popular, easy-to-read biography that focuses on the Queen's personal habits, family life, travels, and relations with the press. Has a chatty tone and tends to idealize the Queen.

Nairn, Tom. *The Enchanted Glass: Britain and Its Monarchy.* London: Radius, 1988. An articulate, scathing critique of the monarchy by a radical political historian. Difficult but interesting reading.

Palmer, Alan W. *Kings and Queens of England.* London: Octopus Books, 1976. An illustrated survey of English monarchs, for young people.

Shows the historical context of each reign, including the impact of
religious strife, the Industrial Revolution, and the two world wars.
Allows for comparison between the Queen's world and that of her
predecessors, such as Elizabeth I and Victoria.

Ross, Stewart. *The Monarchy*. Hove, East Sussex, England: Wayland, 1987.
A concise overview of the history, role, and workings of British
constitutional monarchy, for young readers.
Sunday Express Magazine. *A Week in the Life of the Royal Family*. New
York: Macmillan, 1983. What does the Royal Family actually do? To
answer that question, photographers followed members of the Royal
Family for a week as they performed their duties. Offers
behind-the-scenes detail on royal logistics and protocol.
Ziegler, Philip. *Crown and People*. London: William Collins' Sons, 1978.
A unique, accessible study of popular opinion concerning British kings
and queens since 1900. Includes many quotes from ordinary people at
Elizabeth's Coronation and Silver Jubilee, excerpts from letters to
anti-monarchist Willie Hamilton, and explanations of the pros and cons
of monarchy.

Media Resources

Elizabeth II: Winds of Change. Video/16mm film, 24 minutes. Nielsen-Ferns, 1980. Distributed by Learning Corporation of America. A survey of the Queen's reign, intended for high school and college students, from the series Leaders of the Twentieth Century: Portraits of Power.

Elizabeth R. Video, 120 minutes. British Broadcasting Corporation, 1992. Distributed for sale by Videofinders. Produced to commemorate the fortieth anniversary of the Queen's accession to the throne, this documentary focuses on her working life over the course of a year.

Queen Elizabeth II. 16mm film, 26 minutes. Wolper Productions, 1962. Distributed by Sterling Educational Films. Focuses on the Queen's early life, marriage, and coronation.

Royal Silver Jubilee. Video, 26 minutes. Journal Films, n.d. Distributed by Journal Films. Assesses the Queen's first twenty-five years on the throne, including changes in the monarchy.

Royal Wedding: HRH The Prince Andrew and Miss Sarah Ferguson. Video, 100 minutes. BBC-TV, 1986. Distributed by Films Inc. A chance to witness the pomp and pageantry of a royal wedding. Complete coverage of the wedding procession and service in Westminster Abbey.

Who Shot the Woodcock? Video/16mm film, 50 minutes. Toronto, Canada: CTV Television Network, 1976. Distributed by CTV. Traces British history from the glory of empire to economic decline in the 1970's. From the Windows on the World series, for middle school and high school students.

INDEX

111